For my father, Xsii Ligi'insxw, and my mother, Sa'anx gwanks, who shared much about survival, love, culture, and life with me.

—H.G. / B.D.H.

For my family

—N.D.

THE GRIZZLY MOTHER

By Hetxw'ms Gyetxw (Brett D. Huson)

Illustrated by Natasha Donovan

HIGHWATER
PRESS

Awakening

A warm breeze breaks the cool, dark silence. It carries the scent of moistened soil. A slow heartbeat begins to pulse a little faster. Nox Lik'i'ns x̱w, the grizzly mother, awakens from torpor.[1] Her first-born cubs gnaw and scratch at her, impatient to explore outside of their den. The little bears only know darkness and scent.

[1] **Torpor** is a state of lowered bodily activity in response to cold.

The grizzly mother is exhausted from six months of living in their mountainside den. She has been without food and water for the duration, while also nursing her two cubs since the new year began.

It is early spring, the time of Wiihlaxs, the Black Bear Walking Moon. Hlaphl maaxws, the deep snow that covers the opening to the grizzly mother's den, is melting from the inside. The cold no longer pierces their door, and the earth is beginning to thaw. The air is different and even the grizzly mother now waits impatiently at the entrance, where she can smell the welcome scent of spring.

Once Nox̱ Lik'i'nsx̱w is comfortable to leave, the journey to the food below will be a long one. Unlike the smax̱, black bears, who make their dens lower and closer to the valleys, the grizzly mother digs her den high on the mountainside. Of all the bears, grizzly mothers build their dens at the highest elevations.[1]

¹ The **salmon run** is when salmon migrate from the ocean to the rivers where they were born in order to spawn (release their eggs).

A Shared Land

It is now Lasa 'wiihun, the Fisherman's Moon, which happens during the month of July for the Gitxsan. After gathering and preparing berries for winter, the Gitxsan people begin to move to their fishing camps in preparation for the salmon run.¹ The grizzly mother has been feeding on the valley grasses and sharing the berry patches with the people who live along Xsan, the River of Mists.

Nox̱ Lik'i'nsx̱w is ever cautious. The first few years of a cub's life present some of the hardest struggles they will face. Although many cubs do not survive to become adults, this is the second summer her cubs have had together.

The scents of huckleberries, pine, and cedar imprint[1] on the cubs. While their eyes come to know the mountains, their noses explore miles beyond what they can see.

¹ **Imprint** means to fix permanently (in the memory).

Nox̱ Lik'i'ns̱w and the cubs have an insatiable[1] hunger. They move across their vast territory in search of berry patches, groundhog burrows, and fishing holes. On occasion, the grizzly mother will take down larger prey.[2] Their omnivorous[3] diet benefits the land. They prevent small animals from overgrazing. They also scatter nutrients and seeds, which helps with the renewal of surrounding forests.

[1] **Insatiable** means impossible to satisfy.

[2] A **prey** animal is hunted or killed by another animal for food.

[3] **Omnivorous** means eating both plants and animals.

A Final Run

Lasa lik'i'nxsw, the Grizzly Bear's Moon, has arrived. Three years have now passed, and Nox̱ Lik'i'nsx̱w has been able to keep both her cubs alive to see their third run of miso'o, the sockeye salmon. It is August, and the leaves begin to turn a golden yellow. The Gitxsan have their nets in the river, while their smokehouses fill the sky with a familiar scent.

On the way to their favourite fishing spot,
the grizzly mother and her cubs encounter an old
male who attacked them the previous summer. This
time, he does not pay them any attention. His focus is
on his favourite spot at the top of the waterfall. If they
stay back, they will keep out of harm's way. With a
steep climb and a walk through thick brush, the
grizzly mother and her cubs arrive at the small
gravel beach where they've fished before.

¹ **Metabolism** is the
chemical process
that turns food
into energy.

After spending the past few months gorging themselves on berries and salmon, No̱x Lik'i'ns̱xw and her cubs feel the air change as Lasa gwineekxw, the Getting-Used-to-Cold Moon arrives. This is November. Their metabolisms[1] have slowed, and in one week, they will move as much as a tonne of soil to make their den. This will be the last winter the grizzly mother dens with her first two cubs. Next year, she will send the brother and sister off to begin their own solitary journeys.

The Gitxsan

The Gitxsan Nation are Indigenous peoples from their unceded territories of the Northwest Interior of British Columbia. This 35,000 square kilometres of land cradles the headwaters of Xsan or "the River of Mist," also known by its colonial name, the Skeena River. The land defines who they are.

The Nation follows a matrilineal line, and all rights, privileges, names, and stories come from the mothers. The Lax Seel (Frog), Lax Gibuu (Wolf), Lax Skiik (Eagle), and Gisghaast (Fireweed) are the four clans of the people. It is taboo to marry a fellow clan member, even when there are no blood ties.

The four clans are divided among the territories by way of the Wilp system. A Wilp, or "house group," is a group comprising one or more families. Each Wilp has a head chief and wing chiefs, who are guided by Elders and members of their Wilp. Currently, there are 62 house groups, and each governs their portion of the Gitxsan Territories.

The Gitxsan Moons

K'uholxs	Stories and Feasting Moon	January
Lasa hu'mal	Cracking Cottonwood and Opening Trails Moon	February
Wihlaxs	Black Bear's Walking Moon	March
Lasa ya'a	Spring Salmon's Returning Home Moon	April
Lasa 'yanja	Budding Trees and Blooming Flowers Moon	May
Lasa maa'y	Gathering and Preparing Berries Moon	June
Lasa 'wiihun	Fisherman's Moon	July
Lasa lik'i'nxsw	Grizzly Bear's Moon	August
Lasa gangwiikw	Groundhog Hunting Moon	September
Lasa xsin laaxw	Catching-Lots-of-Trout Moon	October
Lasa gwineekxw	Getting-Used-to-Cold Moon	November
Lasa 'wiigwineekxw or Lasa gunkw' ats	Severe Snowstorms and Sharp Cold Moon	December
Ax wa	Shaman's Moon	a blue moon, which is a second full moon in a single month

Stekyodin

Bulkley River

Kispiox River

Skeena River

**Canada Council
for the Arts**

We acknowledge the support of the Canada Council for the Arts.
Nous remercions le Conseil des arts du Canada de son soutien.

HighWater Press gratefully acknowledges the financial support of the Province of Manitoba through the Department of Sport, Culture and Heritage and the Manitoba Book Publishing Tax Credit, and the Government of Canada through the Canada Book Fund (CBF), for our publishing activities.

HighWater Press is an imprint of Portage & Main Press.
Printed and bound in Canada by Friesens
Design by Relish New Brand Experience
Cover Art by Natasha Donovan

Library and Archives Canada Cataloguing in Publication

Title: The grizzly mother / by Hetxw'ms Gyetxw (Brett D. Huson) ; illustrated by Natasha Donovan.
Names: Huson, Brett D., author. | Donovan, Natasha, illustrator.
Description: Series statement: Mothers of Xsan
Identifiers: Canadiana (print) 20190087277 | Canadiana (ebook) 20190087315 | ISBN 9781553797760 (hardcover) | ISBN 9781553797784 (iPad fixed layout) | ISBN 9781553797777 (PDF)
Subjects: LCSH: Grizzly bear—Life cycles—Juvenile literature. | LCSH: Grizzly bear—British Columbia—Juvenile literature. | LCSH: Gitxsan Indians—British Columbia—Juvenile literature.
Classification: LCC QL737.C27 H87 2019 | DDC j599.784—dc23

22 21 20 19   1 2 3 4 5

www.highwaterpress.com
Winnipeg, Manitoba
Treaty 1 Territory and homeland of the Métis Nation